I0103844

Will Converse Wood

Webster on Protection

Embracing Numerous Extracts from his Speeches

Will Converse Wood

Webster on Protection
Embracing Numerous Extracts from his Speeches

ISBN/EAN: 9783337397838

Printed in Europe, USA, Canada, Australia, Japan

Cover: Foto ©Suzi / pixelio.de

More available books at **www.hansebooks.com**

WEBSTER ON PROTECTION

EMBRACING

NUMEROUS EXTRACTS FROM HIS SPEECHES

BY

REV. WILL C. WOOD, A. M.,

Author of "Protection Constitutional," "The Five Points of Protection," "Five Problems of State and Religion," "Art and Character," "Heaven Once a Week," (Edinburgh Prize Essay) and Various Historical and Critical Essays.

BOSTON
PUBLISHED BY THE HOME MARKET CLUB
1894

CONTENTS.

WEBSTER AND PROTECTION.

BY REV. WILL C. WOOD, A. M.

Webster was a Cyclopean builder of whatever he purposed and planned to build. He used granite boulders, whether he shaped and piled them into structures, or flung them from his catapults. Plymouth Rock and Bunker Hill were fit places and themes for his massive eloquence. His "Reply to Hayne" is a specimen of his mighty building.

In the grand and final debate on protection, before the American people, the next decade, or possibly prolonged through a quarter of a century before general conviction shall have been reached upon this important, this essential question — the protection and prosperity of a nation's industries — the opinions of such a giant mind as Webster's will be worthy of thoughtful consideration.

What did Webster build upon the subject of protection? This question, so interesting to Americans, especially at this period when the tariff is coming up for a new study, we will try to study and present.

Autobiography is likely to be the truest biography, at least in a sincere person. Webster himself, on several occasions, made statements of a growth, of a change of his opinions on this great subject. One of these statements, in 1838, in reply to John C. Calhoun, is in these frank and plain terms :—

When He Opposed Protection and Why He Changed.

[Reply to Calhoun, U. S. Senate, March 22, 1838.]

' I will state the facts, for I have them in my mind somewhat more fully than the honorable member has himself presented them. Let us begin at the beginning. In 1816, I voted against the tariff law which then passed. In 1824, I again voted against the tariff law which was then proposed, and which passed. A majority of New England votes, in 1824, were against the tariff system. The bill received but one vote from Massachusetts; but it passed. The policy was established. New England acquiesced in it, conformed her business and pursuits to it; embarked her capital, and employed her labor, in manufactures; and I certainly admit, that from that time I have felt bound to support interests thus called into being, and into importance, by the settled policy of the Government. I have stated this often, here, and often elsewhere.

" As to the resolutions adopted in Boston, in 1820, and which resolutions he has caused to be read, and which he says he presumes I prepared, I have no recollection of having drawn the resolutions, and do not believe I did. But I was at the meeting, and what I said on that occasion was produced here, and read in the Senate, years ago.

" The resolutions, Sir, were opposed to the commencing of a high tariff policy. I was opposed to it, and spoke against it — the city of Boston was opposed to it — the Commonwealth of Massachusetts was opposed to it. Remember, Sir, that this was in 1820. This opposition continued till 1824. The votes all show this. But, in 1824, the question was decided; the Government entered upon the policy; it invited men to embark their property and their means of living in it. Individuals thus encouraged have done this to a great extent; and therefore, I say, so long as the manufactures shall need reasonable and just protection from Government, I shall be disposed to give it to them. What is there, Sir, in all this, for the gentleman to complain of? Would he have us always oppose the policy, adopted by the country, on a great question? Would he have minorities never submit to the will of the majorities?

" I remember to have said, Sir, at the meeting in Faneuil Hall, that protection appeared to be regarded as incidental to revenue, and that the incident could not be carried fairly above the principal; in other words, that duties ought not to be laid for the mere object of protection. I believe that if the power of protection be inferred only from the revenue power, the protection could only be incidental.

" But I have said in this place before, and I repeat now, that Mr. Madison's publication, after that period, and his declaration that the convention did intend to grant the power of protection, under the commercial clause, placed the subject in a new and a clear light. I will add, Sir, that a paper drawn up apparently with the sanction of Dr. Franklin, and read to a circle of friends in Philadelphia, on the eve of the assembling of the convention, respecting the powers which the proposed new Government ought to possess, shows, perfectly plainly, that in regulating commerce, it was expected Congress would adopt a course which should protect the manufactures of the North. He certainly went into the convention himself under that conviction.*

" Well, Sir, and now what does the gentleman make out against

---

* This remarkable paper of nearly 4,000 words is given as an Appendix to Webster's speech at the convention at Andover, November 9, 1843; the reader will find it in Webster's Works, vol. II, 186–189, with a foot note which says : " The paper from which these extracts are given is published in the American Museum, vol. I, p. 432, with the name of Tench Toxe, Esq., as its author. It is also incorporated into his work called " View of the United States of America, p. 4."

Webster's reference to this paper and Franklin's connection with it, in this Andover speech, is in this paragraph :

" Gentlemen, a native of Massachusetts, certainly inferior to none in sagacity and whose name confers honor upon the whole country, Dr. Benjamin Franklin, in 1787, indicated his sentiments upon these points in a very remarkable manner. The convention to deliberate upon the formation of the Constitution was held in Philadelphia, in May, 1787. Dr. Franklin was, if I remember right, the President, as the office was then called, of Pennsylvania, and was chosen also as a member of the convention. As the delegates were assembling, he invited them to a meeting at his house, on which occasion a paper on this subject was read, which was subsequently printed, and to extracts from which I would call your attention. They will show you what were the sentiments of Dr. Franklin. They prove that far-sighted sagacity, which could discern what was then visible to so few eyes; and that wisdom, which pointed out a course so greatly beneficial."

" At the time these opinions were sanctioned by Dr. Franklin, and indeed, till a very recent period, the manufacturers of the country were shop-workmen ; tailors, hatters, smiths, shoemakers, and others, who wrought in their own shops; but still the principle is the same as if they were banded into corporations."

Extracts from the Paper Approved by Franklin.

" Our money absorbed by a wanton consumption of imported luxuries, a fluctuating paper medium substituted in its stead, foreign commerce extremely circumscribed, and a federal government not only ineffective, but disjointed, tell us indeed too plainly, that further negligence may ruin us forever."

" The commerce of America, including our exports, imports, shipping, manufactures and fisheries, may be properly considered as forming one interest."

me in relation to the tariff? What laurels does he gather in this part
of Africa? I opposed the policy of the tariff, until it had become the
settled and established policy of the country. I have never questioned
the constitutional power of Congress to grant protection, except so far
as the remark made in Faneuil Hall goes, which remark respects
only the length to which protection might properly be carried, so far
as the power is derived from the authority to lay duties on imports.
But the policy being established, and a great part of the country
having placed vast interests at stake in it, I have not disturbed it; on
the contrary, I have insisted that it ought not to be disturbed."

A Free Trader's Criticism.

A biographical author of our day, a free trader, reckless in
historical statement and criticism, ventures these sentences con-

---

"The communication between the different ports of every nation is a business
entirely in their power. The policy of most countries has been to secure this
domestic navigation to their own people."

"Such encouragement to this valuable branch of commerce [fisheries] as
would secure the benefits of it to our own people, without injuring our other
essential interests, is certainly worth attention. The convention will probably
find, on consideration of this point, that a duty or prohibition of foreign
articles, such as our own fisheries supply, will be safe and expedient."

"Though it is confessed that the United States have full employment for all
their citizens in the extensive field of agriculture, yet we have a valuable body
of manufacturers already here, and as many more will probably emigrate from
Europe, who will choose to continue at their trades, and as we have some
citizens so poor as not to be able to effect a little settlement on our waste lands,
there is a real necessity for some wholesome general regulations on this head."

"Another inducement to some salutary regulations on this subject will be
suggested by considering some of our means of conducting manufactures.
Unless business of this kind is carried on, certain great *natural powers* of the
country will remain inactive and useless. Our numerous mill-seats, for
example, by which flour, oil, paper, snuff, gun-powder, iron-work, woollen
cloths, boards and scantling, and some other articles, are prepared, or perfected,
would be given by Providence in vain."

"The encouragement to agriculture afforded by some manufactories is a
reason of solid weight in favor of pushing them with industry and spirit."

"A further encouragement to manufactures will result from improvements
and discoveries in agriculture. There are many raw materials that could be
produced in this country on a large scale, which have hitherto been very
confined."

"If the facts and observations in the preceding part of this paper are
admitted to be true and just, and if we take into consideration with them the
acknowledged superiority of foreign commerce and the fisheries over our manufactories, we may come to the following conclusions:—

"That the United States of America cannot make a proper use of the natural
advantages of the country, nor promote her agriculture and other lesser
interests, without manufactures; that they cannot enjoy the other attainable
benefits of commerce and the fisheries, without some general restrictions and
prohibitions affecting foreign nations."

"It will not be amiss to draw a picture of our country, as it would really
exist under the operation of a system of national laws formed upon these
principles. While we indulge ourselves in the contemplation of a subject at
once so interesting and dear, let us confine ourselves to substantial facts, and

cerning Webster's change of opinion on the tariff. He is speaking of Webster's opposition to Clay's Compromise Act in 1833:
"Webster objected to the horizontal rate, and to an attempt to pledge future Congresses. He was now reduced, after having previously made some of the most masterly arguments ever made for free trade, to defend protection by such devices as he could. Now he derided Adam Smith and the other economists. He first paltered with his convictions on the tariff, and broke his moral stamina by so doing. Many of the people who have been so much astonished at his sudden apostasy on slavery would understand it more easily if their own judgment was more open to appreciate his earlier apostasy on free trade."—[Wm. G. Sumner, "Life of Andrew Jackson."

This is a tissue of misrepresentation. Luther might as well be accused of insincerity in the great religious change of his

---

avoid those pleasing delusions into which the spirits and feelings of our countrymen have too long misled them.

"In the foreground we should find the mass of our citizens the cultivators, (and what is happily for us, in most instances, the same thing), the independent proprietors, of the soil. Every wheel would appear in motion that could carry forward the interests of this great body of people, and bring into action the inherent powers of the country. A portion of the produce of our land would be consumed in the families or employed in the business of our manufacturers, a further portion would be applied in the sustenance of our merchants and fishermen and their numerous assistants, and the remainder would be transported by those that could carry it at the lowest freight (that is, with the smallest deduction from the aggregate profits of the business of the country) to the best foreign markets.

"On one side we should see our manufacturers encouraging the tillers of the earth by the consumption and employment of the fruits of their labors, and supplying them and the rest of their fellow citizens with the instruments of their occupations, and the necessaries and conveniences of life, in every instance where it could be done without injuriously and unnecessarily increasing the distress of commerce, the labors of the husbandmen, and the difficulties of changing our native wilds into scenes of cultivation and plenty. Commerce, on the other hand, attentive to the general interests, would come forward with offers to range through foreign climates in search of those supplies which the manufacturers could not furnish but at too high a price, or which nature has not given us at home, in return for the surplus of those stores that had been drawn from the ocean or produced by the earth."

" The foundations of national wealth and consequence are so firmly laid in the United States, that no *foreign* power can undermine or destroy them. But the enjoyment of these substantial blessings is rendered precarious by domestic circumstances. Scarcely held together by a weak and half-formed federal constitution, the powers of our national government are unequal to the complete execution of any salutary purpose, foreign or domestic."

" I have ventured to hint at prohibitory powers, but shall leave that point, and the general power of regulating trade, to those who may undertake to consider the political objects of the convention, suggesting only the evident propriety of enabling Congress to prevent the importation of such foreign commodities as are made from our own raw materials. When any article of that kind can be supplied at home, upon as low terms as it can be imported, a manufacture of *our own produce*, so well established, ought not by any means to be sacrificed to the interests of foreign trade, or subjected to injury by the wild speculations of ignorant adventurers."

life. "Masterly arguments for free trade,"—mostly one speech, that of 1824, a strong enough speech from the free trade point of view, but not a masterly, nor wholly consistent speech, mainly the development of statements and principles of English economists, a speech such as this comparatively youthful orator might make, from his studies of books, and from his connections with commercial New England. "Derided the economists,"— of the English school, that is; not Edward I., nor Cromwell, nor Colbert, nor Frederick the Great, nor Napoleon, nor Hamilton, nor any other who really ever made a nation great, though Webster did respectfully suggest that "his friends, McCulloch and Senior," did not appreciate American conditions. "Apostasy on free trade," "apostasy on slavery," "broke his moral stamina;" only a complete anamorphosis of facts and right reason could produce such statements, which should forever shame the writer from using the quill again. In Webster's strenuous defence of protection, and of Jackson against Nullification — nullification of the tariff, be it observed, Southern nullification — he was as far as from pole to pole from the mood of compromise with the South or care for personal consequences, which some think came over him a score of years later. In fact, he told Clay he did not believe in his Compromise; "it was time to test the strength of the Union." No, Webster stood, at this time, like the Mount Washington of his native State, granite, unmovable. The South, certainly, felt, at this time, no compliance in the urbane belligerency of his speech. Calhoun, certainly, discerned no quiver of bending in his lofty plume. His horn was exalted. "Defend protection by such devices as he could;"—and yet we venture to say that it would be hard to find a more compact mass of deliverances on the tariff, steadily in one direction, with more of direct vision into the facts and principles, with more indications of conviction of what he uttered, than in the speeches of Daniel Webster, extending over a period of twenty years, some of them conveying his sense of the magnitude and importance and vital concern of the subject to his countrymen, in such a manner as at times to be positively solemn.

His Economic Evolution.

And surely, there were adequate and sufficient reasons for that change of Webster, and for the permanence of that change. First, and more superficially, the revolution or transition in the interests and policy of his New England constituency, after 1824, from commercial to manufacturing pursuits, and then, too, the fact that the Whig party, then formed, to which Webster allied himself, promulgated protection and nailed it to the masthead for its perpetual policy. But then, there were deeper reasons for the profound change in his convictions, not only in his growing maturity of statesmanship, but also in the very facts and principles in the matter—the increasing belief that his great compatriot and compeer, Clay, had been intuitively right and broadly statesmanlike in his one persistent and consistent asseveration that protection and internal improvements were the "American System," resented by Webster at first, but fully seconded by him later ; the fact that Hamilton, Franklin, Dallas, Calhoun, his great compeer of Carolina, and all the Presidents down to Jackson and including him, had declared protection the true American policy ; the very influential fact with Webster, the two letters of Madison to Cabell in 1828, and the later publication of Madison's papers, with his view of the constitutional grounds of protection in the "commercial regulations" phrase, and in connection therewith Webster's wider historical studies as to the extraordinary industrial ferment at the time of the Constitution's formation, which demanded protection as the prime or one of the prime things to be secured by that instrument, and which labor rejoiced at as having been secured and guaranteed therein ; then, too, a clearer discernment of what the younger Webster, with many another inexperienced statesman, was unaware of, the more than rivalry, the hostility, the perpetual hostility, and, considering her insular position and colonial dependencies, the necessary hostility of Great Britain (until she shall revolutionize her policy) to our manufactures, to the manufactures of every other rival also, the world over ; and coupled with this a clear sense, a growing conviction, that without protection on our part that hostility must inevitably be successful and crushing to us, until or unless we shall be willing

—as Webster would never have us, and resisted always—to submit our labor to the underpaid conditions of European labor; observation, furthermore, of the effects of the successive tariffs of his time and of the hostile modifications of the tariff, like ebbs and flows of the tide; and withal, a sense which Calhoun was one of the first and weightiest to express, in 1816, Webster then being present in the Senate, that protection was calculated to be one of the strongest bonds to bind together into one the distant parts of our Union, an idea by no means losing its potency with Webster, but growing and hardening, the rather, as he saw Calhoun later, repudiating and scouting that very protection in behalf of a constituency that would not allow its labor to enter manufactures, and determined to wreck the Union if they could not nullify protection : all these considerations and influences, besides others, cleared Webster's vision, expanded his view, and brought his judgment to rest on deeply grounded conviction. In his speeches after 1824, and increasingly, an expert on protection can see that, in the words of the Scotch phrase, Webster "kens what he is talking aboot."

Clay's American System.

Webster, it is true, came to his final convictions on protection in a different way from Henry Clay. Clay's mind seems to have leaped to the conception of the "American System" with the inspiration of genius; unless, possibly, that great man, Chancellor George Wythe of Virginia, one of the "Signers," and Clay's master in law, may have, sometime, dropped into his fertile mind the germ idea of it; or, unless, again, possibly he may have caught it from Hamilton's great "Report." But the grand idea seems to be Clay's own; and indeed, while in the Kentucky House, young Clay had moved that the whole legislature clothe themselves in American goods; and, as early as 1810 he made his first speech in the United States Senate on "American Manufactures." "Mr. Clay was but a young man," says one, "when he had pretty much matured his 'American System.' It was a comprehensive, gigantic conception, opening a new era in the political history of the country." The conception sprang full-formed, like Minerva from the head of Jove. But Webster, more deliberate in the movements of his mind, like " a mammoth, treading at an equable and stately pace, his native cane-brake," was also precluded from an instantaneous conception of the "American System" by the veil of the agricultural and commercial surroundings of his early manhood, and by his favorite English economists. But, as we have seen, broader ideas of the American position developed conviction, no less deep because more slowly formed, in a direction quite different from the economic impressions and theories of his earlier years.

Webster's mind seems, in one respect, to have changed front along the very line of the interesting Revolutionary story which he told at Pittsburg in 1833. He passed, in a word, from the exclusive commercial view to take, also, the manufacturer's view.

" Some of the States," says Webster, "attempted to establish their own partial systems, but they failed. Voluntary association was resorted to, but that failed also. A memorable instance of this mode of attempting protection, occurred in Boston. The ship-owners, seeing that British vessels came and went freely, while their own ships were rotting at the wharves, raised a committee to address the people, recommending to them, in the strongest manner, not to buy or use any articles imported in British ships. The chairman of this committee was no less distinguished a character than the immortal John Hancock. The committee performed its duty powerfully and eloquently. It set forth strong and persuasive reasons why the people should not buy or use British goods, imported in British ships. The ship-owners and merchants having thus proceeded, the mechanics of Boston took up the subject also. They answered the merchants' committee. They agreed with them cordially, that British goods, imported in British vessels, ought not to be bought or consumed; but then they took the liberty of going a step further, and of insisting, that *such goods ought not to be bought or consumed at all* (Great applause). 'For,' said they, 'Mr. Hancock, what difference does it make to us, whether hats, shoes, boots, shirts, handkerchiefs, tinware, brass-ware, cutlery, and every other article, come in British ships, or come in your ships; since, in whatever ships they come, they take away our means of living?' " (Speech at Pittsburg, Penn., July 9, 1833.)

Before 1825, Webster talked for commercial New England; after that, for the manufactures, for all the industries, of the whole Union.

Webster, though a man naturally proud of his consistency,
fully set his seal of approval on his change of opinions as late
as 1846 :—

"Mr. President, if it be an inconsistency to hold an opinion upon
a subject at one time, and in one state of circumstances, and to hold a
different opinion upon the same subject at another time, and in a
different state of circumstances, I admit the change. Nay, Sir, I will
go further ; and, in regard to questions which, from their nature, do
not depend upon circumstances for their true and just solution, I mean
constitutional questions, if it be an inconsistency to hold an opinion
to-day, even upon such a question, and on that same question, to hold
a different opinion a quarter of a century afterwards, upon a more
comprehensive view of the whole subject, with a more thorough
investigation into the original purp. ses and objects of that Constitution,
and especially after a more thorough exposition of those objects and
purposes by those who framed it, and have been trusted to administer
it, I should not shrink even from that imputation. I hope I know
more of the Constitution of my country than I did when I was twenty
years old. I hope I have contemplated its great objects more broadly.
I hope I have read with deeper interest the sentiments of the great
men who framed it. I hope I have studied with more care the condition of the country when the convention assembled to form it."

List of Webster's Tariff Speeches.

Webster's speeches which deal with protection are these :—

Speech of 1814, mentioned by Lodge, and the famous one in Faneuil Hall in 1820, neither of which have we seen.

Speech in U. S. Senate, 1824.

These belong to the "English" or free trade period. All the
rest are made for the American policy ; from 1824 on, Webster
stood everywhere and always for protection.

Second Speech on the Tariff, U. S. Senate, May 9, 1828.

Two Speeches on Foot's Resolution, Replies to Hayne, Jan. 20
and 26, 1830.

Speech at National Republican Convention, Worcester, Mass., 1832.

Reply to Calhoun, U. S. Senate, Feb. 16, 1833.

Speech at Buffalo, June, 1833.

Speech at Pittsburg, July 8, 1833.

On Surplus Revenue, U. S. Senate, May 31, 1836.

Reduction of Duty on Coal, U. S. Senate, Feb. 24, 1837.

Sub-Treasury Speech, U. S. Senate, March 12, 1838.

Reply to Calhoun, March 22, 1838.

At Niblo's Saloon, New York, March 15, 1838.
General Effects of Protection, March 3, 1840.
On Treasury Note Bill, Reply to Calhoun, March 30, 1840.
Saratoga Mass Meeting, Aug. 19, 1840.
Reception at Boston, Sept. 30, 1842.
Andover Convention, Nov. 9, 1843.
Albany Mass Meeting, Aug. 27, 1844.
Whig Convention, Philadelphia, Oct. 1, 1844.
Convention at Valley Forge, Oct. 3, 1844.
Against the Walker Tariff, U. S. Senate, July 25, 27, 1846.
Public Dinner, Philadelphia, Dec. 2, 1846.
Speech before Election, Faneuil Hall, Oct. 24, 1848.

The object of this pamphlet is to group Webster's utterances
on the tariff, for the convenient study and reference of the
American people, to most of whom they will probably come
with almost the force of a revelation and to all with the strength
of prophecy. The compiler's only claim to merit is in allowing
Webster to speak for himself, rather than in attempting to speak
for him, and in bringing together for the first time specimen ex-
cerpts from his great speeches during the twenty years of his
greatest intellectual vigor and political influence, upon a subject
as much in issue to-day as it was then and to the understanding
of which nothing that is recent contributes more than these
luminous passages from the past.

Protection, the Original American Policy.

Webster maintained, in opposition to Calhoun, that protection
is the Original American Policy. The passage is extended,
but foundational. It is part of his reply to Calhoun, "The
Constitution Not a Compact," in the United States Senate, Feb.
16, 1833.

"Sir, the world will scarcely believe that this whole controversy,
and all the desperate measures which its support requires, have no
other foundation than a difference of opinion upon a provision of the
Constitution, between a majority of the people of South Carolina on
one side, and a vast majority of the whole people of the United States
on the other." "It was incredible and inconceivable, that South
Carolina should thus plunge headlong into a resistance to the laws on
a matter of opinion, and on a question in which the preponderance of
opinion, both of the present day and of all past time, was so over-

whelmingly against her." "Sir, what will the civilized world say, what will posterity say, when they learn that similar laws have existed from the very foundation of the Government; that for thirty years, the power was never questioned; and that no State in the Union has more freely and unequivocally admitted it than South Carolina herself?"

The Motive of Protection Does Not Vitiate the Tariff.

"The great object of all these laws is, unquestionably, *revenue.* If there were no occasion for revenue, the laws would not have been passed; and it is notorious that almost the entire revenue of the country is derived from them. And, as yet, we have collected none too much revenue. The treasury has not been more reduced for many years than it is at the present moment. All that South Carolina can say is, that in passing the laws which she now undertakes to nullify, *particular imported articles were taxed, from a regard to the protection of certain articles of domestic manufacture, higher than they would have been, had no such regard been entertained.* And she insists that, according to the Constitution, no such discrimination can be allowed; that duties should be laid for revenue, and revenue only; and that it is unlawful to have reference, in any case, to protection. In other words, she denies the power of Discrimination. She does not, and cannot, complain of excessive taxation; on the contrary, she professes to be willing to pay any amount for revenue, merely as revenue; and up to the present moment there is no surplus of revenue. Her grievance, then, that plain and palpable violation of the Constitution which she insists has taken place, is simply the exercise of the power of Discrimination. Now, Sir, is the exercise of this power of discrimination plainly and palpably unconstitutional?

"I have already said that the power to lay duties is given by the Constitution in broad and general terms. There is also conferred on Congress the whole power of regulating commerce, in another distinct provision. Is it clear and palpable, sir,— can any man say it is a case beyond doubt —that under these two powers Congress may not justly *discriminate, in laying duties, for the purpose of countervailing the policy of foreign nations, or of favoring our own home productions?* Sir, what ought to conclude this question forever, as it would seem to me, is, that the regulation of commerce and the imposition of duties are, in all commercial nations, powers avowedly and constantly exercised for this very end. That undeniable truth ought to settle the question; because the Constitution ought to be considered, when it uses well-known language, as using it in its well-known sense. But it is equally undeniable that it has been, from the very first, fully believed that this power of discrimination was conferred on Congress; and the Constitution was itself recommended, urged upon the people, and enthusiastically insisted on in some of the states, for that very reason. Not that at that time the country was extensively engaged in manufactures, especially of the kinds now existing. But the trades and crafts of the seaport towns, the business of the artisans and manual laborers, those employments the work in which supplies so great a portion of the daily wants of all classes — all these looked to the new Constitution as a source of relief from the severe distress which followed the war. It would, sir, be unpardonable, at so late an hour, to go into details on this point, but the truth is as I have stated. The papers of the day, the resolutions of public meetings, the debates in the conventions, all that we open our eyes upon in the history of the times prove it."

Webster shows that Calhoun misapprehended two incidents claimed to support his view; one was that "a power to protect manufactures was expressly proposed, but not granted." Webster shows that the proposition Calhoun had in mind was "'to establish public institutions, rewards and immunities' for the promotion of manufactures and other interests. The convention," adds Webster, "supposed it had done enough — at any rate it had done all it had intended — when it had given to Congress, in general terms, the power to lay imposts and the power to regulate trade." Webster says that Calhoun also misunderstood Mr. Martin, that he objected before the Maryland legislature that the Constitution did not contain protection; Webster shows that Martin's complaint was only that the power of protection had been taken away from the separate States.

How the First Tariff (1789) Was Passed.

"I find," continues Webster, "that, having provided for the administration of the necessary oaths, the very first measure proposed for consideration is the laying of imposts; and in the very first committee of the whole into which the House of Representatives ever resolved itself on this, its earliest subject, and in this, its very first debate, the duty of so laying the imposts as to encourage manufactures, was advanced and enlarged upon, by almost every speaker, and doubted or denied by none. The first gentleman who suggests this as the clear duty of Congress, and as an object necessary to be attended to, is Mr. Fitzsimons, of Pennsylvania; the second, Mr. White, of Virginia; the third, Mr. Tucker, of South Carolina.

"But the *great* leader, Sir, on this occasion, was Mr. Madison. Was *he* likely to know the intentions of the convention and the people? Was *he* likely to understand the Constitution?

"At the second sitting of the committee, Mr. Madison explained his own opinions of the duty of Congress, fully and explicitly. I must not detain you, Sir, with more than a few short extracts from these opinions, but they are such as are clear, intelligible, and decisive.

" ' The states,' says he, ' that are most advanced in population, and ripe for manufactures, ought to have their particular interest attended to, in some degree. While these states retained the power of making regulations of trade they had the power to cherish such institutions. By adopting the present Constitution, they have thrown the exercise of this power into other hands; they must have done this with an expectation that those interests would not be neglected here.' "

Attitude of South Carolina.

"In the same debate, Sir, Mr. Burk, from South Carolina, supported a duty on hemp, for the express purpose of encouraging its growth on the strong lands of South Carolina. ' Cotton' he said, ' was also in contemplation among them, and if good seed could be procured, he hoped might succeed.' Afterwards, Sir, the cotton seed was obtained, its culture was protected, and it did succeed. Mr. Smith, a very distinguished member from the same state, observed: ' It has been said, and justly, that the states which adopted this Constitution expected its administration would be conducted with a favorable hand. The manufacturing states wished the encouragement of manufactures; the maritime states, the encouragement of ship-building; and the agricultural states, the encouragement of agriculture.' "

"And how, Sir, did this debate terminate? What law was passed? There it stands, Sir, among the statutes, the second law in the book. It has a *preamble*, and that preamble expressly recites that the duties which it imposes are laid ' for the support of Government, for the discharge of the debts of the United States, and *the encouragement and protection of manufactures.*' Until, Sir, this early legislation, thus coeval with the Constitution itself, thus full and explicit, can be explained away, no man can doubt of the meaning of that instrument in this respect.

"Mr. President, this power of *discrimination*, thus admitted, avowed, and practised upon, in the first revenue act, has never been denied or doubted until within a few years past. It was not at all doubted in 1816, when it became necessary to adjust the revenue to a state of peace. Certainly, South Carolina did not doubt it. The tariff of 1816 was introduced, carried through, and established, under the lead of South Carolina. Even the *minimum* policy is of South Carolina origin. The honorable gentleman himself supported, and ably supported, the tariff of 1816. He has informed us, Sir, that his speech on that occasion was sudden and off-hand, he being called up by the request of a friend. I am sure the gentleman so remembers it, and that it was so; but there is, nevertheless, much method, arrangement, and clear exposition in that extempore speech. It is very able, very, very much to the point, and very decisive. And in another speech, delivered two months earlier, the honorable gentleman had declared ' that *a certain encouragement ought to be extended, at least to our woolen and cotton manufactures.*' " " Sir, it is no answer to say that the tariff of 1816 was a revenue bill. So are they all revenue bills. The point is, and the truth is, that the tariff of 1816, like the rest, did *discriminate;* it did lay duties for protection. Look to the case of coarse cottons, under the minimum calculation; the duty on these was sixty to eighty per cent. Something besides revenue, certainly, was intended in this; and, in fact, the law cut up our whole cómmerce with India in that article.

" It is, Sir, only within a few years that Carolina has denied the constitutionality of these · protective laws. The gentleman himself has narrated to us the true history of her proceedings on this point. He says that after the passing of the law of 1828, despairing then of being able to abolish the system of protection, political men went forth among the people, and set up the doctrine that the system was unconstitutional. ' *And the people,*' says the honorable gentleman, ' *received the doctrine.*' This I believe is true, Sir. The people did then receive the doctrine; they had never entertained it before. Down to that period, the constitutionality of these laws had been no more doubted in South Carolina, than elsewhere. And I suspect it is true, Sir, and I deem it a great misfortune, that to the present moment, a great portion of the people of the state have never yet seen more than one side of the argument. I believe that thousands of honest men are involved in scenes now passing, led away by one-sided views of the question, and following their leaders by the impulses of an unlimited confidence. Depend upon it, Sir, if we can avoid the shock of arms, a day for reconsideration and reflection will come; truth and reason will act with their accustomed force, and the public opinion of South Carolina will be restored to its usual Constitutional and patriotic tone.

"But, Sir, I hold South Carolina to her ancient, her cool, her un-
influenced, her deliberate opinions. I hold her to her own admissions,
nay, to her own claims and pretensions, in 1789, in the first Congress,
and to her acknowledgments and avowed sentiments through a long
series of succeeding years. I hold her to the principles on which she
led Congress to act, in 1816; or, if she have changed her own opinions, I claim some respect for those who still retain the same opinions.
I say she is precluded from asserting, that doctrines which she has
herself so long and so ably sustained, are plain, palpable and danger-
ous violations of the Constitution."

Protection the Historical Fact.

At the Albany mass meeting, Aug. 27, 1844, amid a score of
pages on protection, historical and argumentative, Webster
says :—

"This sentiment, gentlemen, continued to prevail through all the
administrations which followed General Washington. It was regarded
by Mr. Jefferson as a just principle of legislation, as he stated in the
beginning of his administration in 1802, and still more distinctly just
before the expiration of his term of office in 1808. I need not say
that everybody knows that Mr. Madison, in 1810, 1812 and 1816,
reiterated all these sentiments.

"This is the history of the country on the great question of protection. I speak of the *fact*, and assert it as an historical truth, proved
from the journals of Congress, the messages of the Presidents, the acts
of legislation, beginning with the second law ever passed and running
through successive administrations, that it was held as the undoubted
right of Congress, and no more the right than the duty, by just discrimination, to *protect the labor of the American people.*"

"I am for reciprocity treaties," says Webster. "No, I will not
say treaties, but arrangements; for the whole power over the subject
lies with Congress, and not with the treaty-making power."

The Voice of Faneuil Hall in 1785 and the Green Dragon Tavern in 1788.

[Speech at Andover Convention, Nov. 9, 1843.]

"Now, gentlemen, it so happened, that in the years of severe disas-
ter between the peace and the formation of the Constitution, the merchants and mechanics of Boston had their attention called to the
subject, and their proceedings, only a little earlier than the paper just
referred to, [that of Tench Toxe, Esq., read at Franklin's house]

sprang from the same sense of necessity. I will trouble you to listen to some of them which I gather from the publications of that day.

"At a numerous and respectable meeting of ' the merchants, traders and others, convened at Faneuil Hall,' on Saturday, the 16th of April, 1785, the following, among other resolutions, were adopted :—

" 'Whereas, certain British merchants, factors and agents from England are now residing in this town, who have received large quantities of English goods, and are in expectation of receiving further supplies, imported in British bottoms, or otherwise, greatly to the hinderance of freight in all American vessels," etc., "we the merchants, traders, and others of the town of Boston, do agree,—

" 'First, that a committee be appointed to draft a petition to Congress representing the embarrassments under which the trade now labors, and the still greater to which it is exposed; and that the said committee be empowered and directed to write to the several seaports in this State, requesting them to join with the merchants in this town in similar applications to Congress, immediately to regulate the trade of the United States agreeably to the powers vested in them by the government of this commonwealth," etc.

"That the said committee be requested to write to the merchants in the several seaports of the other United States, earnestly recommending to them an immediate application to the legislatures of their respective States to vest such powers in Congress (if not already done) as shall be competent to the interesting purposes aforesaid, and also to petition Congress to make such regulations as shall have the desired effect.' "

" So far the merchants. Now what said the mechanics, the artisans, the shop-workmen, to this? At an adjourned meeting of persons belonging to those classes at the Green Dragon Tavern, on Monday, the 25th day of April, 1785, the following resolutions, among others, were passed : —

" 'Voted, that a committee be appointed by this body to draft a petition to the next General Court, setting forth the difficulties the manufacturers of this town labor under by the importation of certain articles (to be enumerated in the petition) and praying a prohibition, or that such duties may be laid as will effectually protect the manufacture of the same.

" 'Voted, that we do bear our public testimony against sending away our circulating cash for foreign remittances, as this practice, we conceive, is calculated to impoverish the country.' "

" Well, how did the merchants receive this? I will show you. Here is a letter, signed in their behalf, by that great patriot and prince of merchants, John Hancock.

BOSTON, MAY 2, 1785.

" 'GENTLEMEN,—Your communications of the 26th ult. were interesting and agreeable. Our situation is truly critical. To the United States in Congress we look for effectual relief, and to them we have accordingly appealed.

" 'We shall cheerfully use what influence we have in promoting and encouraging the manufactures of our country, etc.

" 'We derive great support from that unanimity which appears to actuate our respective proceedings, and while that subsists, we can no more despair of the commerce, trade, and manufactures than of the liberties of America.'

John Hancock.

"This state of things continued till 1788, when the Massachusetts convention to consider the Constitution was held in Boston. Some of the most eminent persons who have shed lustre on the State were members of that convention, and many of them, as is well known, felt great doubts about adopting the Constitution. Among these were two individuals, none other than John Hancock and Samuel Adams, the proscribed patriots. But the energy, determination, perseverance and earnestness of the mechanics and tradesmen of Boston influenced even these wise and great men, and tended to, and did in an eminent degree, contribute to the ratification of the Constitution. Any man will see this who will look into the public transactions of that day.

"There was a particular set of resolutions, founded on this very idea of favoring home productions, full of energy and decision, passed by the mechanics of Boston. And where did the mechanics of Boston meet to pass them? Full of the influence of these feelings, they congregated at the headquarters of the Revolution. I see, waving among the banners before me that of the Old Green Dragon. It was there, in Union Street, that John Gray, Paul Revere, and others of their class, met for consultation. There, with earnestness and enthusiasm, they passed their resolutions. A committee carried them to the Boston delegation in the convention. Mr. Samuel Adams asked Colonel Revere how many mechanics were at the meeting; and Colonel Revere answered, ' More than there are stars in heaven.'

" The resolutions had their effect. The Constitution was established; and a universal burst of joy from all classes, merchants, manufacturers and mechanics, proclaimed the exultation of the people at the thrice-happy event."

" This ' grand procession ' took place; and the artisans, mechanics, and manufacturers of Boston, together with the merchants and other classes, indulged in the hope, not more sanguine than the event warranted, that under the operation of the new national Constitution, prosperity would return, business revive, cheerfulness and contentment spread over the land, and the country go forward in its career of growth and success."

" But, Gentlemen, this sentiment and feeling were not merely the sentiment and feeling of Massachusetts. We may look at the debates in all the state conventions, and the expositions of all the greatest men in the country, particularly in Massachusetts and Virginia, the great Northern and Southern stars, and we shall find it everywhere held up as the main reason for the adoption of the Constitution, that it would give the general government the power to regulate commerce and trade."

The New Era of 1825.

[Faneuil Hall, April 3, 1825.]

" Let me rather say that in regard to the whole country a new era has arisen. In a time of peace the proper pursuits of peace engage society with a degree of enterprise and intenseness of application heretofore unknown. New objects are opening and new resources developed on every side. We tread on a broader theatre, and if, instead of acting our parts according to the novelty and importance of the scene, we waste our strength in mutual crimination and recrimination concerning the past, we shall resemble those navigators who, having escaped from some crooked and narrow river to the sea, now that the whole ocean is before them should, nevertheless, occupy themselves with the differences which happened as they passed along among the rocks and the shallows, instead of opening their eyes to the wide horizon around them, spreading their sail to the propitious gale that woos it, raising their quadrant to the sun and grasping the helm with the conscious hand of a master."

England Not Our Model — Capital and Labor.

At the public dinner at Philadelphia, Dec. 2, 1846, Webster endorsed Massachusetts resolutions :—

"My object is, and has been," said he, " in everything connected with the protective policy, the true policy of the United States, to see that the labor of the country, the industry of the country, is properly provided for. I am looking, not for a law such as will benefit capitalists — they can take care of themselves — but for a law that shall induce capitalists to invest their capital in such a manner as to occupy and employ American labor. Now, on this subject, I shall hand to the gentlemen of the press a series of resolutions passed in Massachusetts which entirely embody my own sentiments."

" I will only say, that I am for protection, ample, permanent, founded on just principles; and that, in my judgment, the principles of the act of 1842 are the true principles,— *specific* duties, and not *ad valorem* duties ; just discrimination, and in that just discrimination, great care not to tax the raw material so high as to be a bounty to the foreign manufacturer and an oppression on our own. Discrimination and specific duties, and such duties as are full and adequate to the purposes of protection,— these are the principles of the act of 1842."
" My object is to obtain, in the best way I can, and when I can, and as I can, full and adequate and thorough protection to the domestic industry of the country, upon just principles."

" Gentlemen, on the tariff I have spoken so often and so much, that I am sure no gentleman wishes me to utter the word again. There are some things, however, which cannot be too often repeated. Of all countries in the world, England, for centuries, was the most tenacious in adhering to her protective principles, both in matters of commerce and manufacture. She has of late years relaxed, having found that her position could afford somewhat of free trade. She has the skill acquired by long experience, she has vast machinery and vast capital, she has a dense population; a cheaply working, because a badly fed and badly clothed, population. She can run her career, therefore, in free trade. We cannot, unless willing to become badly fed and clothed, also. Gentlemen, for the gymnastic exercises, men strip themselves naked; and for this strife and competition in free trade, our laborers, it seems, must strip themselves naked, also."

Duty of Government, and Why the Union Was Formed.

In his great speech at the Whig Convention at Philadelphia, Oct. 1, 1844, Webster unfurled the Whig flag.

" The Whig party maintains the propriety of protecting, by custom-house regulations, various pursuits and employments among ourselves. Our opponents repudiate this policy, and embrace the doctrines of what is called free trade. This is the general party line. The distinction is not a local but a party distinction."

" Gentlemen, incidental protection, which some persons, just now, would represent as transcendental protection, what is it? It is no protection at all, and does not deserve the name. It is a result which comes, if it comes at all, without design, without certainty, and without discrimination. It falls on tea and coffee, as well as on iron and broadcloth. Let us not be deluded by such a thin and flimsy pretext. It is an insult to our understandings."

" There is not an operative nor a workingman, who is not interested in, and supported by the protective laws of the Government. Protection touches every man's bread. If ever, then, there was a subject worthy of the attention of a public man or a statesman, it is this of protection."

" The Federal Government, I say, fails in its duty to Pennsylvania, and in its duty to every other state in this Union, if it lets the power lie latent, and refuses to use it. That is the pinch, the very exigence, that made this Government of the United States. For that, Massachusetts came into it; for that, Pennsylvania came into it. The power

of protection was in both States. It existed on all sides. The compact was made, to give it identity, universality, union, and that is all
we want."

"But the time is now come when the policy of a reasonable, permanent protection must be settled (A voice in the crowd, "Now or
never!") I say, *Now or never!* It is a question that is most exciting
to the whole country, and absolutely vital to the interests of the people of Pennsylvania; and it is ' Now or NEVER!'"

Protection Against European Labor.

[Speech at Pittsburg, Penn., July 8, 1833.]

"I am in favor of protecting American manual labor; and, after
the best reflection I can give the subject, and from the lights which I
can derive from the experience of ourselves and others, I have come
to the conclusion that such protection is just and proper; and that,
to leave American labor to sustain a competition with that of the
over-peopled countries of Europe, would lead to a state of things to
which the people could never submit. This is the great reason why
I am for maintaining what has been established. I see at home, I see
here, I see wherever I go, that the stimulus, which has excited the
existing activity, is producing the existing prosperity of the country, is
nothing else than the stimulus held out to labor by compensating prices.
I think this effect is visible everywhere, from Penobscot to New Orleans,
and manifest in the condition and circumstances of the great body of the
people; for nine-tenths of the whole people belong to the laborious,
industrious, and productive classes; and on these classes the stimulus
acts. We perceive that the price of labor is high, and we know that
the means of living are low; and these two truths speak volumes in
favor of the general prosperity of the country."

"Be assured, gentlemen, that nothing can advance the mass of
society, in prosperity and happiness, nothing can uphold the substantial interest, and steadily improve the general condition and
character of the whole, but this one thing, *compensating rewards to
labor*. The fortunate situation of our country tends strongly, of
itself, to produce this result; the Government has adopted the policy
of co-operating with this natural tendency of things; it has encouraged
and fostered labor and industry, by a system of discriminating duties;
and the result of these combined causes may be seen in the present
circumstances of the country."

"It certainly appears to me, gentlemen, to be quite evident, at this
time, and in the present condition of the world, that it is necessary to
protect the industry of this country against the pauper labor of England,

and other parts of Europe. An American citizen, who has children to maintain, and children to *educate*, has an unequal chance against the pauper of England, whose children are not to be educated, and are probably already on the parish; and who himself is half fed and clothed by his own labor, and half from the poor-rates, and very badly fed and clothed after all."

Coal and Labor — Artisans Made the Constitution.

[Reduction of Duty on Coal, U. S. Senate, February 24, 1837.]

" Considering what has been the former course of Congress on this subject, it is as clear a proposition as can be stated that the interest of the poor required the continuance of the tax. Whether we look to the debates of the convention or to the earliest acts of the Federal Government, we shall perceive that it was admitted to be proper and necessary to levy a duty on imported coal. One of the very first articles enumerated in the first revenue law is foreign coal. The protection of the domestic article was warmly advocated at that time by the Virginia delegation, as an obvious duty of the new government.

" The honorable member thinks that Congress, by taking off this tax, would give the exclusive power of keeping up the price to American producers. I differ from him in opinion. I think that, by taking off this tax, we shall give that power to British producers and make our citizens the victims of their extortions." " Ah, but the member is for the protection of labor. Very true. And I insist that the protective policy of the United States is aimed point blank at the protection of labor. Do not the poor of our cities warm themselves over coal fires? What glowing pictures, or, rather, what shivering pictures of suffering have been presented to the Senate in the eloquent descriptions (if he thinks them eloquent) of the honorable gentleman from South Carolina! [Preston.] But was not the laboring class in our cities the very first who received the protection of this Government? The first demand of a Constitution was for their protection. It was the operatives, spread along the Atlantic coast, whose voices brought the Constitution into being. It was not the voices of Hancock and Adams, but of Paul Revere and his artisans which most efficiently advocated the movement for independence. It was the pouring in of a flood of foreign manufactures that gave the first impulse towards the adoption of a Constitution for our own protection: and has not the labor of our whole country been protected under it to this day? Have not the laboring classes of the United States their life, and breath, and being, under that instrument?"

" But it becomes enlightened legislators to take a different view of the subject. The true way to protect the poor is to protect their labor. Give them work and protect their earnings; that is the way to benefit the poor. Our artisans, I repeat it, were the first to be protected by the Constitution. The protection extended, under our laws, to capital was as nothing to that which was given to labor; and so it should be. Since, in the year 1824, I stood upon this ground, I have retained the same position, and there I mean to stand. The free labor of the United States deserves to be protected, and so far as any efforts of mine can go, it shall be. The gentleman from Connecticut (Niles) tells us that coal is a bounty of Providence; that our mountains are full of it; that we have only to take hold of what God has given us. Well, Sir, I am for protecting the man who does take hold of it; who bores the rock; who penetrates the mountain; who excavates the mine, and by his assiduous labor, puts us into practical possession of this bounty of Providence. It is not wealth while it lies in the mountain. It is human labor which brings it out and makes it wealth. I am for protecting that poor laborer whose brawny arms thus enrich the state. I am for providing him with cheap fuel, that he may warm himself and his wife and children."

" I know very well that many of the citizens of Boston have applied to have this tax diminished, and, if I thought it could with propriety be done, I would cheerfully do it. Some petitions, too, have been presented from one of our fishing towns; but they ought to remember that all bounties on the fisheries, as well as this duty on coal, rest upon one great basis of mutual concession for the protection of labor, and for the benefit especially of the operative classes of society. And whoever says that this is a system which favors capital at the expense of the poor, misrepresents its advocates, and perverts the whole matter, from A to Z."

" My object is, to make coal cheap—*permanently* cheap; cheap to the poor man as well as the rich man; and to that end we shall arrive, if the laws are suffered to take their course. But to meddle with them, in the existing state of things, is the very worst thing that can be done, either for poor or rich."

The Farmer's Interest.

At the convention at Valley Forge, Oct. 3, 1844, Webster said :—

" The protective system is a favorite measure with you, with us at home, and with all our party. We deem it a most necessary system, one that cannot, under any circumstances, be dispensed with, as being necessary to the comfort, necessary to the happiness, the prosperity of all; and vitally touching the permanent, as well as the present, interests of the community."

"There are many false prophets going to and fro in the land, who declare that the tariff benefits only the manufacturer, and that it injures the farmer. This is all sheer misrepresentation.

"Every farmer must see that it is his interest to find a near purchaser for his produce, to find a ready purchaser, and a purchaser at a good price. Now, the tariff supposes, that if there be domestic manufactures carried on successfully, there will inevitably be those engaged therein who will consume a large amount of agricultural products, because they do not raise any for themselves,— a new class of consumers of the farmer's commodities, an enlarged class of customers."

Wages and Prices — Seth Peterson.

Intelligent free traders admit that wages lower under free trade, but insist that prices will lower, *pari passu;* and a day's wages will buy as much as under the high wages of protection. The New York *Commercial Bulletin*, of Nov. 17, 1892, says: "If workmen concede in wages, they will get their full compensation in the cheapening of the products they have to buy, so that the net result to the earner is the same under lower wages as under higher."

This is plainly fallacious. Hundreds of thousands are not wage-earners, but stipendiaries, with inherited property, or men who cannot spend the interest of their acquired property, or men with fixed salaries. These men, spenders of millions, get twice as much service for their money, while the million that serve them get half pay. Futhermore, a ten per cent. cut means more to a laborer than to a salaried man.

But let us hear *Seth Peterson*, as brought forward by Webster to speak on this interesting topic :

[Saratoga Mass Meeting, Aug. 19, 1840.]

"I have in my hand an extract from a speech in the House of Representatives of a zealous supporter, as it appears, of the administration, who maintains, that, other things being reduced in proportion, you may reduce the wages of labor without evil consequences. And where does he seek this example? On the shores of the Mediterranean. He fixes upon Corsica and Sardinia. But what is the Corsican laborer, that he should be the model upon which American labor is to be formed? Does he know anything himself? Has he any education, or does he give any to his children? Has he a home, a freehold, and the comforts of life around him? No; with a crust of bread and a handful of olives, his daily wants are satisfied. And yet, from such a state of society, the laborer of New England, the laborer of the United States, is to be taught submission to low wages."

"There is not much danger that schemes and doctrines such as these shall find favor with the people. They understand their own interest too well for that. Gentlemen, I am a farmer on the seashore, and have, of course, occasion to employ some degree of agricultural labor. I am sometimes, also, rowed out to sea, being, like other New England men, fond of occasionally catching a fish, and finding health and recreation in warm weather from the air of the ocean. For the few months during which I am able to enjoy this retreat from labor, public or professional, I do not often trouble my neighbors, or they me, with conversation on politics.

"It happened, however, about three weeks ago, that on such an excursion as I have mentioned, with one man only with me, I mentioned this doctrine of the reduction of prices and asked him his opinion of it. He said he did not like it. I replied, 'the wages of labor, it is true, are reduced; but then, flour and beef, and perhaps clothing, all of which you buy, are reduced also. What, then, can be your objections?' 'Why,' said he, 'it is true that flour is now low, but then, it is an article that may rise suddenly, by means of a scanty crop in England or at home; and, if it should rise from five dollars to ten, I do not know for certain that it would fetch the price of my labor up with it. But while wages are high, then I am safe; and if produce chances to fall, so much the better for me. But there is another thing. I have but one thing to sell, that is my labor; but I must buy many things — not only flour, and meat, and clothing, but also some articles that come from other countries — a little sugar, a little coffee, a little tea, a little of the common spices, and such like. Now, I do not see how these foreign articles will be brought down by reducing wages at home, and before the price is brought down of the only thing I have to sell, I want to be sure that the prices will fall also, not of a part but of all the things that I must buy.'

"Now, gentlemen, though he will be astonished or amused, that I should tell the story before such a vast and respectable assemblage as this, I will place this argument of *Seth Peterson*, sometimes farmer and sometimes fisherman on the coast of Massachusetts, stated to me while pulling on an oar with each hand, and with the sleeves of his red shirt rolled up above his elbows, against the reasonings, the theories, and the speeches, of the administration, and all its friends, in or out of Congress, and take the verdict of the country, and of the civilized world, whether he has not the best side of the question.

" Since I have adverted to this conversation, gentlemen, allow, me to say that this neighbor of mine is a man fifty years of age, one of several sons of a poor man; that by his labor he has obtained some few acres, his own unencumbered freehold, has a comfortable dwelling, and plenty of the poor man's blessings. Of these, I have known six, decently and cleanly clad, each with the book, the slate, and the map, proper to its age, all going at the same time daily to enjoy the blessing of that which is the great glory of New England, the common free school. Who can contemplate this, and thousands of other cases like it, not as pictures, but as common facts, without feeling how much our free institutions, and the policy hitherto pursued, have done for the comfort and happiness of the great mass of our citizens. Where in Europe, where in any part of the world, out of our own country, shall we find labor thus rewarded, and the general condition of the people so good? Nowhere; nowhere! Away, then, with the injustice, and the folly, of reducing the cost of productions with us to what is called the common standard of the world! Away, then, away, at once and forever, with the miserable policy, which would bring the condition of a laborer in the United States to that of a laborer in Russia or Sweden, in France or Germany, in Italy or Corsica! Instead of following these examples, let us hold up all our own, which all nations may well envy, and which, unhappily, in most parts of the earth, it is easier to envy than to imitate."

How Free Trade Raises Prices.

[Reply to Calhoun, March 3, 1840.]

" The object, and I think the effect, of the tariff of 1828, was not so much to raise prices high, as it was to keep the market steady, to give some check to the extravagant amount of foreign importations, and some security that labor should receive a reasonable reward. This is all that was asked. The great abundance of capital abroad, the low rate of interest, and the great sacrifices which were willingly made in Europe for the purpose of prostrating our establishments, called for some security and protection, or we were not likely to maintain competition. And we are always to remember that when our own manufactures shall be prostrated by the extremely low prices of imported goods, we shall be obliged immediately to pay extremely

high prices for those same imported goods. The fact undoubtedly is, that under the process of protection, the common price or
cost of goods has become less. No one can deny that. Everybody knows that goods are both better and cheaper. A man's labor
will buy more for him than it would. This is the effect of competition.
If we take out of the market the products of our own labor, who does
not see that prices would rise enormously? Let this be tried on any
article. Take away, for instance, all American made hats and shoes;
would not the article be immediately doubled in price? Reasonable
protection does not so much raise the price of labor, although it
should raise it in some degree, as it multiplies the modes of its
employments. It prevents any particular channel from being filled
and choked up. One of the secrets of prosperity is, that there shall be
a considerable variety in the pursuits and labors of men. I fear our
Southern friends do not feel the full influence of this important truth.
For my part, as a well-wisher to the South, I should be glad to know
that there were manufactures, such as are suited to their wants, the
nature of their labor, and their general condition, in every county,
from this place to the Gulf of Mexico."

Protected Labor Can Consume.
[Reply to Calhoun, March 3, 1840.]

" When labor is employed, labor can consume ; when it is not employed, it cannot consume. Who buys the pork and the lard of the
Northwestern states? Who takes the corn of North Carolina and
Virginia, and the flour of the latter state? Is it not the North and the
East? Virginia and Carolina have no better customer than Massachusetts. To say nothing of the amount of naval stores received from
North Carolina, and used by the navigating interest of the East, let
me only refer to breadstuffs. Two millions of bushels of corn, and
four hundred thousand barrels of flour, have been imported into the
single city of Boston in one year. Most of this corn is from North
Carolina and Virginia, and much of the flour from Virginia. I find
it has been estimated that upwards of *six millions of dollars* have
been paid by Massachusetts for breadstuffs imported in a single year.
All this is consumed and paid for by employed labor. Take away
employment for our labor, or drive it from its accustomed pursuits,
and its power of consumption is at an end."

Protection and Importation.
[Reply to Calhoun, March 3, 1840.] ·

" But not only does the protection of labor in the North and East
enable it to buy the products of the South, but all protection of labor

increases general consumption. Hence we find that the manufacture of many useful articles at home does not diminish the aggregate amount of importations. This is a very important truth, and all our history confirms it. I have looked at the tables of exports and imports, from the very first origin of the Government, and I do not find anything to countenance the idea that imports, in the aggregate, fall off in consequence of protecting labor at home. There were quite as great fluctuations forty or forty-five years ago, as there have been since the tariff of 1824. A well-employed and prosperous community can buy and consume. This is the solution of the whole matter, and the whole science of political economy has not one truth of half so much importance as this."

Webster was sagacious to discriminate between a large healthful importation, which comes from the desire of well-paid labor to " get the best" in lines in which we may be excelled by foreigners, and a large unhealthful importation, of men driven to purchase abroad because manufactures are stifled at home, this latter importation a constant drain, of course, on the country.

Extravagant Importation.
[Speech on Treasury Note Bill, March 30, 1840.]

"Mr. President, our imports, the last year, reached the unprecedented amount of one hundred and fifty-seven millions of dollars, exceeding by nearly fifty millions the import of the year before. Yet even this seems not to satisfy us all. Public men appear to have ruling passions or strong tendencies of preference towards particular objects. It seems to me that our Government, and many of our people, have imbibed an extravagant and morbid love of importation. They seem to judge of the prosperity of the country, and the happiness of its people, exclusively by the quantities of foreign merchandise which they annually consume. With all respect, the President himself, I think, has feelings with this tendency."

"Mr. President, it is remarkable that this spirit of importation should become so strong just when our own occupations and employments are most depressed. The cotton manufactures, practically, are in a worse state than they have been for twenty years. It is supposed that at least one-half of the woolen machinery in the United States has ceased to work, and many of the establishments might be purchased at one-third of their cost. The iron trade and the coal trade suffer with the rest. If the condition of the Eastern and Northern manufacturers be as I have stated, I doubt whether one would receive much more favorable accounts if he were to inquire into the condition of trade and business at Pittsburg, at Wheeling, or at Cincinnati.

" Under the circumstances of the country, Sir, I confess I do not comprehend how any man should desire to see a greater importation of foreign commodities."

" I am for bringing about no reduction in the price of labor. On the other hand, I regard high rates of labor as the surest proofs of general prosperity.

" I have no desire to see a greater or more unrestrained importation of foreign goods. On the contrary, I am for laying a tax on imported luxuries, thus securing an adequate revenue to Government."

Webster illustrates the impoverishment of an exclusively agricultural policy, whose manufactures are killed out by the " British Colonial Policy," as Clay used to designate free trade.

Ireland the Victim of Free Trade.
[Against the Walker Tariff, 1846.]

" But why are the people of Ireland not prosperous, contented, and happy? We hear of a potato panic, and a population in Ireland distressed by the high price of potatoes. Why, Sir, the price of potatoes in this city is three times the price of potatoes in Dublin; and, at this moment, potatoes are twice as dear throughout the United States as throughout Ireland. There are potatoes enough, or food of other kinds. But the people are not able to buy them. And why? That is the, stringent question. Why cannot the people of Ireland buy potatoes or other food? The answer to this question solves the Irish case; and that answer is simply this, the people have not employment. They cannot obtain wages. They cannot earn money. The sum of their social misery lies in these few words. There is no adequate demand for labor."

" But then, this only advances the inquiry to the real question, which is, *Why* are the laboring people of Ireland so destitute of useful and profitable employment?"

" From early times the English government has discouraged, in Ireland, every sort of manufacture, except the linen manufacture of the North. It has, on the other hand, encouraged agriculture."
" This is the reason why labor is nothing, and can produce nothing but mere physical living, until the system shall be entirely changed. This constitutes the great difference between the state of things in Europe and America. In Europe, the question is, how men can live? With us, the question is, how well they can live? Can they live on wholesome food, in commodious and comfortable dwellings?

Can they be well clothed, and be able to educate their children?
Such questions do not arise to the political economists of Europe.
When reasoning on such cases as that of Ireland, the question with
them is, how physical being can be kept from death? That is all."

Protection and Good Citizenship.

[Speech at Buffalo, June, 1833.]

"My sentiments, gentlemen, on the tariff question, are generally
known. In my opinion, a just and a leading object in the whole
system is the encouragement and protection of American manual labor. I confess that every day's experience convinces me more and
more of the high propriety of regarding this object. Our Government is made for all, not for few. Its object is, to promote the greatest good of the whole; and this ought to be kept constantly in view in
its administration. The far greater number of those who maintain
the Government belong to what may be called the industrious or productive classes of the community. With us, labor is not depressed,
ignorant, and unintelligent. On the contrary, it is active, spirited,
enterprising, seeking its own rewards, and laying up for its own competence and its own support. The motive to labor is the great stimulus to our whole society; and no system is wise or just which does
not afford this stimulus, as far as it may. The protection of American labor against the injurious competition of foreign labor, so far, at
least, as respects general handicraft productions, is known, histori-
cally, to have been one end designed to be obtained by establishing
the Constitution; and this object and the Constitutional power to ac-
complish it, ought never to be surrendered or compromised in any
degree.

"Our political institutions, gentlemen, place power in the hands of
all the people; and to make the exercise of this power, in such hands,
salutary, it is indispensable that all the people should enjoy, first,
the means of education, and second, the reasonable certainty of pro-
curing a competent livelihood by industry and labor. These institutions are neither designed for, nor suited to, a nation of ignorant
paupers. To disseminate knowledge, then, universally, and to secure
to labor and industry their just rewards, is the duty, both of the General and State Governments, each in the exercise of its appropriate
powers. To be free, the people must be intelligently free; to be
substantially independent, they must be able to secure themselves
against want, by sobriety and industry; to be safe depositaries of
political power, they must be able to comprehend and understand the
general interests of the community, and must themselves have a stake,

in the welfare of that community. The interest of labor, therefore, has an importance, in our system, beyond what belongs to it as a mere question of political economy. It is connected with our forms of government and our whole social system. The activity and prosperity which at present prevail among us, as every one must notice, are produced by the excitement of compensating prices to labor; and it is fervently to be hoped that no unpropitious circumstances, and no unwise policy, may counteract this efficient cause of general competency and public happiness."

Protection and the South.

Webster, like Clay, fully believed that protection was good for the whole country; for the South, as well as the North. He believed the South Carolina politicians were deluded and deluding in their representations of the injurious effects of the tariff on their section. He gave facts and arguments several times.

[Reply to Calhoun, March 3, 1840.]

" If the South can sell her cotton, or part of it, to New England, for the same prices, it is as well for her as to sell it all to Old England. Her income depends on the price, not on the place of sale. If an export of sixty millions is reduced to an export of forty millions, in consequence of there having been found a market at home for twenty millions, it is not only no worse for the South, but it is, in truth, much better. This is perfectly plain; and I must confess it has always appeared to me to be the strangest thing in the world that our Southern friends should look with jealousy and ill-will on a market rising up in the North and East for their own great staple; thus not only giving them the general advantage of another large market — which advantage is itself always great — but giving them the additional advantage of a nearer market, and a more certain and steady market, because not so liable to be disturbed, either by the political events, or commercial contingencies of Europe. I have inquired much into the subject, and I find that intelligent merchants in New Orleans and Mobile regard the home market as of very great importance to the cotton planter. The Eastern demand, they say, comes in early, takes away the first part of the crop, and helps, therefore, to fix the price, and to fix it high. Some have estimated this advantage as equivalent to two cents on the pound of cotton. All must see, I think, that it is a clear and great advantage, and I wish the subject might be calmly considered and weighed by the honorable member from South Carolina and his friends."

We shall find a fact to match the statement above in the later speech, where, within two years after the South got the free trade tariff they clamored for, in 1846, cotton had fallen to about half the price per pound.

[Speech on the Tariff, U. S. Senate, July 27, 1846.]

" Sir, it does not become me to do more than suggest in what the interests of other parts of the country appears to me to consist." " It appears to me the plainest proposition in the world, that there is nothing which the whole South can so profitably turn its attention to as the manufacture of these coarse cotton fabrics. The South might soon come to undersell New England altogether, because it is a fabric in the value of which the raw material is the most important element. As labor, therefore, forms but a small portion of the article produced in its manufactured state, it requires less capital for machinery and expensive establishments. The raw material being the principal element composing the value, gives, of course, an advantage to those who raise the raw material, and who manufacture it just where it is produced. Now, I must say, that, at the exhibition here, last month, or the month before, nothing appeared to me better done than some of these cheap cotton fabrics from Virginia, North Carolina and Georgia; and I believe, as strongly as I may venture to believe anything against the opinion of men of more local knowledge, that these manufactures will succeed and prosper, if we let them alone, in the Southern States. And I wish them to prosper. They have arisen in a desire on the part of the Southern people to clothe themselves and their people, against New England competition. I conceive it for the interest of every community to produce its own clothing; and it strikes me that the effort on the part of the South ought to be encouraged."

In this friendly suggestion to the South, both as to matter and manner, we seem almost to be listening to the wise and paternal counsel and congratulations to the New South, nearly half a century later, of President Harrison on his memorable Southern tour.

Webster, Clay, Calhoun and Jackson.

Webster disclosed his own deepest convictions as to protection by his personal references to the opinions and conduct of others thereupon.

Clay's Compromise Act of 1833 he opposed in public and private, as needlessly compromising the protective policy to conciliate perverse South Carolina.

Calhoun he gave clearly and courteously to understand that he had perfectly discerned Calhoun's purposes, and that their success would be only temporary.

[Speech on Sub-Treasury Bill, U. S. Senate, March 12, 1838.]

"Now, Sir, I must say that in 1833 I entertained no doubt at all that the design of the gentleman was exactly what he now states. On this point I have not been deceived. It was not, certainly, the design of all who acted with him; but that it was his purpose I knew then as clearly as I know now, after his open avowal of it; and this belief governed my conduct at that time, together with that of a great majority of those in both Houses of Congress, who, after the act of 1824, felt bound to carry out the provisions of that act and to maintain them reasonably and fairly. I opposed the Compromise Act with all my power. It appeared to me every way objectionable; it looked like an attempt to make a new Constitution; to introduce another fundamental law, above the power of Congress, and which should control the authority and discretion of Congress, in all time to come. This, of itself, was a conclusive objection with me; I said so then, have often said so since, and say so now. I said then that I for one should not be bound by that law more than by any other law, except that, as it was a law passed on a very important and agitating subject, I should not be disposed to interfere with it, until a case of clear necessity should arise. On this principle I have acted since. When that case of necessity shall arise, however, should I be in public life, I shall concur in any alteration of that act which such necessity may require. That such an occasion may come I more than fear. I entertain something stronger than a doubt upon the possibility of maintaining the manufactures and industry of this country upon such a system as the Compromise Act will leave us, when it shall have gone through its processes of reduction. All this, however, I leave to the future."

On Jackson's Wobbling Expressions.

[National Republican Convention, Worcester, Oct. 12, 1832.]

President Jackson, too, Webster declaimed against as bending before the storm he had essayed to rule, receding from his previous opinions and votes on protection, and putting forth the Verplanck Tariff, only defeated by the Compromise Act of the

"Great Pacificator." Whether just or unjust, Webster's words disclose his own intense convictions on protection.

" In that compend of Executive opinions in the Veto Message, the whole principle of the protecting policy is plainly and pointedly denounced."

Rarely does Webster use greater sarcasm :

" It would be grateful, if we could contemplate the President of the United States as an identical idea. But even this secondary pleasure is denied us. In looking to the published records of Executive opinions, sentiments favorable to protection, and sentiments against protection, either come confusedly before us, at the same moment, or else follow each other in rapid succession, like the shadows of a phantasmagoria."

He contrasts Jackson's Protection Message of 1830 :

" ' In this conclusion, I am confirmed as well by the opinions of Presidents Washington, Jefferson, Madison and Munroe, who have each repeatedly recommended the exercise of this right under the Constitution, as by the uniform practice of Congress, the continued acquiescence of the States, and the general understanding of the people ; ' " and then Webster's sarcasm takes another turn : "The message of 1830 is a well-written paper ; it proceeded, probably, from the Cabinet proper. Whence the veto of 1832 proceeded, I know not ; perhaps from the Cabinet improper."

The Compromise Tariff of 1833 — The Minimum Principle.

[Distribution of Surplus Revenue, U. S. Senate, May 31, 1836.]

The honorable member from South Carolina has referred to the tariff act of 1828 as the true cause of the swollen state of the treasury. I agree that there were many things unnecessarily inserted in the act of 1828. But we know they were not put there by the friends of the act. That act is a remarkable instance, I hope never to be repeated, of unnatural, violent, angry legislation. Those who introduced it designed, originally, nothing more than to meet the new condition of things which had been brought about by the altered policy of Great Britain in relation to taxes on wool. A bill with the same end in view had passed the House of Representatives in 1827, but was lost in the Senate. The act of 1828, however objectionable though it certainly was in many respects, has not been, in my opinion, the chief cause of the over-product of the customs. I think the act of 1832, confirmed by the act of 1833, commonly called the Compromise Act, has had much more to do in producing that result. Up to the time of the passing of the act of 1832, the minimum principle had been preserved in laying duties on certain manufactures, especially woolen cloths. This ill-understood and much-reviled principle appears to me, nevertheless, and always has appeared to me, to be a just, proper, effectual, and strictly philosophical mode of laying protective duties. It is exactly conformable, as I think, to the soundest and most accurate principles of political economy. It is, in the most rigid sense, what all such enactments, so far as practicable, should be; that is to say, a mode of laying *specific duty*. It lays the impost just where it will do good, and leaves the rest free. It is an intelligent, discerning, discriminating principle; not a blind, headlong, generalizing, uncalculating operation. Simplicity, undoubtedly, is a great beauty in acts of legislation, as well as in the works of art; but in both it must be a simplicity resulting from congruity of parts and adaptation to the end designed; not a rude generalization, which either leaves the particular object unaccomplished, or in accomplishing it, accomplishes a dozen others also, which were not desired. It is a simplicity which is wrought out by knowledge and skill; not the rough product of an undistinguishing, sweeping, general principle.

" Let us suppose that the gradations in woolen cloths be represented by a line. At one end of this line are those of the highest price, and let the scale descend to the other end, where, of course, will be those of the lowest price. Now, with the two ends of this line our manufacturers have not much to do; that is to say, they have not much to do with the production of the very highest, or the very lowest, of these articles. Generally speaking, they work in the intermediate space. It was along this space, along this part of the line of work, that the *minimum* principle, as it has been usually called, operated.* It struck just where the great object of protection required it to strike, and it struck nowhere else. All the rest is left free. It wasted no power. It accomplished its object by the least possible expenditure of means. Its aim was levelled at a distinct and well-discerned object, and its aim was exact, and the object was reached.

---

* William J. Lowndes and John C. Calhoun were both of South Carolina; the one propounded, the other defended, the *minimum* principle. Experience vindicated this South Carolina device as a most effective high duty. U. S. Stats. at large, vol. III. p. 310, chapt. CVII. (1816), "An Act to regulate duties on imports and tonnage;" Horace Greeley, "Political Economy," 323 foll.

"But the *minimum* had become the subject of obloquy and reproach. It was railed at, even, in good set terms, by some who professed to be, and who doubtless were, friends of the protective policy. It was declared to be a deception. It was said that it cheated the people, inasmuch as under its operation, they did not see what amount of taxes they really paid. For one, I did not admit the fact, nor yield to the argument. I had no doubt the people knew what taxes they paid under the operation of the laws, as well as we who passed the laws; and whether they stopped to make precise calculations or not, if they found the tax not oppressive, and the effect of the law decidedly salutary, I did not believe they would complain of it, unless it was made a part of some other controversy. The *minimum* principle, however, in its application to broadcloths, was overthrown by the law of 1832, and that law, as it came from the House of Representatives, and as it finally passed, substituted a general and universal *ad valorem* duty of fifty per cent."

"Now, Mr. President, when we recollect that the duties on woolen fabrics, of all kinds, bring into the treasury four, or five, or six millions a year, every man acquainted with our manufactures must see at once that a portion of this vast sum is perfectly useless as a protective duty; because it is imposed on fabrics with which our manufacturers maintain no competition, and in regard to which, therefore, they ask no protection."

"It is therefore, Sir, that I regard the law of 1832, and not the law of 1828, as the great error in our legislation." "I wish not to discuss the act of 1833. I do not propose, at present, to disturb its operation; but having alluded to it, I take the occasion of saying that I have not the least idea that that act can remain as the settled system of this country. When the honorable member from Kentucky introduced it, he called it a measure of conciliation, and expressed the hope that, if the manufacturing interests should be found to suffer under it, it might be modified by general consent. Although never concurring in the act, I entertain the same hope. I pray most fervently that former strifes and controversies on the tariff question may never be revived; but at the same time, it is my opinion that the principles established by the law of 1833 can never form the commercial system of this country."

Prosperity Under the Tariff of 1842.

[Speech against the Walker Tariff, 1846.]

Probably no protective tariff ever quickened the prosperity of a nation more speedily, more visibly, to the apprehension of everybody, than that of 1842. Webster said in 1846:

" Now, Sir, no man can deny that the course of things in this country, for the last twenty or thirty years, has had a wonderful effect in producing a variety of employments. How much employment has been furnished by the canals and railroads, in addition to the great amount of labor, not only in the factories, rendered so odious in some quarters by calling them monopolies and close corporations, but in the workshops, in the warehouses, on the sea and on the land, and in every department of business! There is a great and general activity in the employments of men amongst us; and that is just exactly what our condition ought to be.

" The interest of every laboring community requires diversity of occupations, pursuits and objects of industry. The more that diversity is multiplied, or extended, the better. And, Sir, take this great truth; place it on the title page of every book of political economy intended for the use of the United States; put it in every Farmer's Almanac; let it be the heading of the column in every Mechanic's Magazine; proclaim it everywhere and make it a proverb, that *where there is work for the hands of men there will be work for their teeth.* Where there is employment there will be bread. It is a great blessing to the poor to have cheap food; but greater than that, prior to that, and of still greater value, is the blessing of being able to buy food by honest and respectable employment. Employment feeds, and clothes, and instructs. Employment gives health, sobriety and morals. Constant employment and well paid labor produce, in a country like ours, general prosperity, content and cheerfulness. Thus happy have we seen the country. Thus happy may we long continue to see it."

Webster stood like an Ajax Telamon, at the age of three score and four, only six years before his death, against

The Robt. J. Walker Tariff of 1846.
[Speech in U. S. Senate, July 25, 1846.]

" Mr. President, it appears strange, but after all, we must admit the fact, that the appearance of this bill in the Senate, with a prospect of its passage, has struck the people generally with surprise. It has brought about no small degree of alarm." " I think it must be the conviction of every person who hears me, who has observed the development of public sentiment, since the introduction of this measure, that the country is surprised, greatly surprised, at any probability that it should receive the final sanction of Congress and the President."

" It is said to be in favor of free trade and against monopoly. But every man connected with trade is against it; and this leads me to ask, and I ask with earnestness, and hope to receive an answer, At whose request, at whose recommendation, for the promotion of what interest, is this measure introduced? Is it for the importing merchants? They all reject it, to a man. Is it for the owners of the navigation of the country? They remonstrate against it. The whole internal industry of the country opposes it. The shipping interest opposes it. The importing interest opposes it. Who is it that calls for it, or proposes it? Who asks for it? Has there been one single petition presented in its favor from any quarter of the country? Has a single individual in the United States come up here and told you that his interest would be protected, promoted, and advanced by the passage of a measure like this? Sir, there is an imperative unity of the public voice the other way, altogether the other way. And when we are told that the public requires this, and that the people require it, we are to understand by the public certain political men, who have adopted the shibboleth of party for the public, and certain persons who have symbols, ensigns, and party flags, for the people, and that's all. I aver, Sir, that is all. I call upon any man who is within these walls, to stand up and tell me what public interest, what portion of men of business; who, amongst all those who earn their living on the sea or on land, in the field of agriculture, or in the workshop of the artisan; who, amongst them all comes up here and asks for such a measure as this? Not a man. If there are any persons out doors in favor of this bill, why, then, Sir, I can only say that silence is contagious, and its friends out doors are as mute as its friends in doors.

"We hear no defence of this bill. An honorable member from South Carolina (Mr. McDuffie) has said that 'the bill vindicates itself.' That is so far true as this, that if it do not vindicate itself, it is not vindicated at all. Nobody here stands sponsor for it. Nobody here answers the objections which are urged against it. I see on the opposite side, Sir, gentlemen of the highest character in this country and of the longest experience in this government, gentlemen who have debated questions great and small, for thirty years, gentlemen properly considered as being amongst those from whom selection is to be made for the highest honors in the gift of the people; and yet on this question, as important, I will undertake to say, as any which has been discussed in Congress from the formation of the Constitution, we hear from those gentlemen not a word, not one single word."

" Now it is not for me to put it to those gentlemen, it is a consideration which, if it arise at all, must arise in their own bosoms, whether they can stake their reputation on this measure, indorsed, as it is by them, and yet make no defence of it?"

" In submitting my views to the Senate, I propose, Sir, in the first place to consider the bill as a measure for making all duties on import- ed goods *ad valorem* duties.

"Secondly, to consider its effects on certain interests supposed to be protected by former and now existing laws.

" Thirdly, I propose to consider its effects upon the navigation and commercial interests of the country, a topic of very deep interest, which has not, as yet, been fully considered in this discussion.

" Fourthly, I propose to consider its effect on the great industrial employments and labor of the people."

Two or three paragraphs from these two great speeches, July 25 and 26, and the supplementary remarks, July 28 :—

"It does appear to me then, that we are to make this alteration in our whole system of revenue, we are to bring this great change over all the departments of private life, we are to produce unknown effects on all the industrial classes of the community, upon a mere theory, an assumption which suggests that all the interests of the country are severely taxed to maintain the manufactures. I must say, Sir, that the notions which prevail in the Treasury Department and in the Ex- ecutive Department appear to me almost insane." "Mr. President, if intelligent men, of patriotic purposes, good intentions, and great respectability in many walks of life, private and public, ever were seized with a monomania, that disease has taken a strong hold of those who come to us with such statements and sentiments as these. How else can we account for such a zeal for over importation ; a zeal which looks for a paradise on earth, if we can only be surrounded with British manufactures without stint and without count. The love of importation has become a sort of passion with those at the head of affairs ; an unthinking, headlong passion."

" There seems to be a sedulous purpose of hostility to the manufac- turing interests." " It does prefer, by its enactment, and in its con- sequences, foreign labor to domestic labor." " I aver it, and I am going to prove it."

" What answer is to be made to all this ? Is it the result of inatten- tion or of culpable ignorance? Are those who framed this bill determined, of purpose, to break down the manufactures of the country, or are they only indifferent and utterly reckless in all that relates to them ?"

"It is not a bill for the people," Webster says again. "It is not a bill for the masses. It is not a bill to add to the comfort of those in middle life, or of the poor. It is not a bill for employment. It is a

bill for the relief of the highest and most luxurious classes of the
country, and a bill imposing onerous duties on the great industrious
masses, and for taking away the means of living from labor everywhere, throughout the land. It cannot be disguised. You cannot
mask its features. No man is so blind as not to see what this bill is;
and the people will not be so callous as not to feel it."

" I repeat it, Sir, that the bill has a face and front, so that when it
is held up to the country, no man need write at the bottom of it,
whether it is a democratic or an aristocratic bill." " It has the face
and front of an aristocratic bill, oppressive of the poor and working
man; and in every respect it corresponds to its face and front."

Specific and Ad Valorem Duties.

Webster's discussion of specific and *ad valorem* duties is a
ne plus ultra of statement and reasoning. The subject needed
no further elucidation then; it needs no further elucidation now.

[Against the Walker Tariff, 1846.]

Webster declares of the "universal *ad valorem* assessment"
of the Walker Tariff, that "that has not been the practice of
the Government at any time during its organization. In every
administration, from that of Washington down, a contrary system has always prevailed." "It has been the sentiment of all
connected with the Government, so far as I know."

Clay being mentioned, Crittenden stated his position on the
Compromise as "*ad valorem* on *Home Valuation*," and Webster proceeded:

"Mr. Clay's proposition, then, was, 'If you will bring the article
here, then I will take that system of valuation.' Well, that proposition and this are wide as the poles apart." "I am glad to find, therefore, that Mr. Clay's authority stands exactly where it should stand,
on such a question as this, in strict conformity with his knowledge,
his experience, and his character."

Webster cited Buchanan's emphatic and well-reasoned argument, in 1842, against *ad valorem* duties :—

"Sir, in the same year (1842), the present Secretary of State
(Mr. Buchanan), in a speech to the Senate, reasoned in the strongest
language, upon the necessity, the absolute necessity of carrying the
principle of specification in laying duties as far as possible.

"'I am not only opposed to any uniform scale of *ad valorem*,
but to any and all *ad valorem* duties, whatever, except where, from

the nature of the article imported, it is not subject to a specific duty. Our own experience has taught us a lesson on this subject which we ought not soon to forget. I cannot refrain from adverting to some of many reasons for this opinion.

" ' Our *ad valorem* system has produced great frauds upon the revenue, whilst it has driven the regular American merchant from the business of importing, and placed it almost exclusively in the hands of British manufacturers.' "

" ' Again, *ad valorem* duties deprive the American manufacturer of nearly all the benefits of incidental protection.' "

" Let us, then, abandon the idea of a uniform horizontal scale of *ad valorem* duties; and, whether the duties be high or low, let us return to the ancient practice of the government. Let us adopt wise discriminations; and, whenever this can be done, impose specific duties.' "

Webster produced the valuable correspondence of Secretary Wm. H. Crawford and the House of Representatives, in 1818, and went on :

" Now, Sir, what is the great fact that makes *ad valorem* duties unsafe as a general principle of finance? I must confess my utter consternation when I heard, the other day, the honorable chairman of the Committee of Finance say that he did not believe that a case of fradulent undervaluation had ever been made out! Why, it is the notoriety of a thousand such cases occurring every year, in this Government, and in all governments where the system of *ad valorem* duties in any degree prevails, and the value is ascertained upon the invoices on proof from abroad; it is the notoriety of a thousand such cases of fraud that has led to the adoption of this general rule, and raised it even into a principle, as I have shown. My friend from Maine (Evans) must have satisfied the honorable chairman, and the Senate, as well as everybody else, of the number and the notoriety of the cases of fraudulent undervaluation, because he enumerated instances, and hundreds of instances, in which goods have been seized and forfeited for undervaluation. The cases are numberless; and, Sir, since the subject has come up, and since persons out doors have heard the declaration of the honorable chairman, my desk has been laboring under the weight of facts communicated from various portions of the commercial community. I will state only a few out of many."

" Can any man gainsay the truth of this? Is there a merchant, foreign or American, in the United States, who will express any contrariety of opinion? Is there a man, high or low, who denies it?"

I know of none; I have heard of none. Sir, it has been the experience of this Government, always, that the *ad valorem* system is open to innumerable frauds. What is the case with England? In her notions favorable to free trade, has she rushed madly into a scheme of *ad valorem* duties? Sir, a system of *ad valorem* duties is not *free* trade, but *fraudulent* trade. Has England countenanced this? Not at all; on the contrary, on every occasion of a revision of the tariff of England, a constant effort has been made, and progress attained, in every case, to augment the number of specific duties, and reduce the number of *ad valorem* duties." " In this British tariff, out of seven hundred and fourteen articles, six hundred and eight are subject to specific duties. Every duty that from its nature could be made specific, is made specific."

At Faneuil Hall, before Taylor's election, in 1848, Webster made one of his last tariff speeches.

The Tariff of 1846 in Review.

[Faneuil Hall, October 24, 1848.]

" The tariff of 1846 is a measure new to the history of the commercial world in modern times. It is a tariff of duties altogether *ad valorem*, with no specifications, with no just discrimination in favor of domestic industry and products. If anybody can find a tariff like that, let it be produced. When under discussion in the Senate, we said all we could against it, and we said some pretty provoking things, but there was not a word uttered in its support. Its friends maintained a most judicious silence. One of them arose, and by an almost unnatural force of speech cried out, ' The tariff will vindicate itself,' and sat down.

" And now, let me ask, after an experience of two years, who is helped by this tariff of 1846,—what portions of the country? It is, in fact, a measure dictated by South Carolina; it is a measure in which the South took the initiative, and led off, and the North, as has been too much its wont, followed. There are men in the North who see the sun in the South, and they think they see all other light there. Now, is South Carolina any richer for this tariff? Now that the tariff is passed, now that we have free trade, said these friends of the new tariff, we shall see Carolina looming up like one of the Southern constellations. She will become rich; she is enfranchised and set at liberty; hereafter, she will take a great lead, and her cotton will enrich her people.

" Pray, what has been the result? When these glowing sentences were on the lips of her eloquent men, her cotton was from ten to eleven cents a pound. Those words had hardly cooled, when, under this protection by free trade, and under this admirable tariff of 1846, which put down all other abominable tariffs, her cotton is down to five and a half and six cents a pound."

"This tariff and sub-treasury have protected them (Pennsylvania) by depressing the price of their main commodity at least one-third."

"A respectable gentleman, well known to you, this afternoon placed in my hands a statement, according to which forty woolen mills, known to him, have, within the last four months, all stopped working, from the pressure of the money market and the influx of foreign manufactures, and they have discharged nearly *three thousand hands*, and greatly reduced the wages of the remainder."

"The tariff, such as it is, is and must be destructive to the great interests of the whole people whether manufacturers or not. I say that, because I see that we cannot stand for any length of time this overwhelming importation of foreign commodities, without an utter derangement of the currency of the country."

"Who is benefited by it? It is all from the unwillingness of party men to acknowledge themselves in error. I appeal to you. You are all acquainted with the state of commerce and business. Do you know twenty men, active in business, sensible men, who do not wish the sub-treasury anywhere but where it is? Do you know twenty mechanics and manufacturers, men of sense and industry, who do not wish the tariff of 1846 had never been born? What is it that keeps it in being but prejudice, party pride and obstinacy? Gentlemen, I have no right to speak here to members of a party to which I do not belong; but yet I would venture to beseech them to consider whether there may not be some considerations—whether our own daily business, the maintenance of our wives and families, the securing of a competence for a comfortable old age,—whether these considerations may not be of more importance than that we should learn by rote, and recite by rote, every dogma of the party to which we are attached?"

Such were Webster's great utterances on the protective policy. These are only specimens, fine but fair. There is nothing which runs counter to them in anything Webster said after 1824. Perhaps another score of similar passages could be produced from his published works and from other printed addresses. From the positions he assumed after he got the true *Point de Vue* of protection, there is no recession, no wavering. Insinuations in certain newspapers might lead their readers to imagine that Webster might have had moments of a return of predilection for some free trade notion or other, some swirl of a backward eddy; but I do not find them. He seems to have outgrown them utterly. I have gleaned carefully all his speeches accessible, and his letters accessible, and can find nothing which shows that he ever glanced back on the free trade on which in 1825 or thereabout he forever turned his back.

Three things strike us in Webster's final attitude on protection :

1. Webster had come to regard the protective policy in the same light as Henry Clay, as, next to the preservation of the Union, the paramount object of American statesmanship. His own expression is, "This question, as important, I will undertake to say, as any which has been discussed in Congress from the formation of the Constitution." Again, at Philadelphia, 1844 : "Protection touches every man's bread. If ever, then, there was a subject worthy the attention of a public man or a statesman, it is this of protection." He grew to appreciate more and more how closely the welfare of the working classes was bound up in it. After paying a tribute to "a country of workingmen who are able, if necessary, to work fourteen hours a day," and "bid defiance to all tariffs," and can "stand upon the strength of their own character, resolution, and capacity," he goes on :

"Not, Sir, that there is one house in New England, at this moment, in which the proceedings of this day are not looked for with intensest interest. No man rises in the morning but to see the newspaper. No woman retires at night without inquiring of her husband the progress of this great measure in Washington. They ask about it in the streets. They ask about it in the schools. They ask about it in the shoemakers' shops, the machine-shops, the tailors' shops, the saddlers' shops, and, in short, in the shops of all artisans and handicrafts. They ask about it everywhere. And they will take whatever answer comes, as men should take it ; and they will feel as men should feel, when they hear it."—*Speech against tariff of 1846.*

And Webster's tones take on the deepest solemnity of appeal, as when, on this same free trade bill of Walker, of 1846, he said :

" I would beseech it (the administration) not to make this leap in the dark in the early part of its career. I would beseech it to stand firm on established ground, on the system on which our revenue now stands; and to lay aside all propositions for extensive and elementary change."

2. Webster occupies a peculiar position, an important position, as Defender of Protection, in one respect, which, so far as I am aware, no one has ever remarked. For a certain important period, Webster, of all the supreme, the Agamemnonian warriors on Protection, held the field alone, namely from the Compromise Act of 1833 to the new Tariff Act of 1842, and perhaps beyond. Calhoun had left the field, receding from his early tariff speech of 1816, one of the most comprehensive and weighty ever made, withdrawing into the swamps of free trade and nullification; and Clay, the "Great Pacificator," had sealed his cannons' mouths by the ten years' truce of his great Compromise. But Webster did not agree to that Compromise; he declared he would not respect it. And for the next ten years, he was, above all others, the one great tariff advocate. Citations are before us from a dozen notable speeches of Webster on the tariff, in the Senate and at mass meetings, between 1833 and 1846. This was by no means an unimportant period; Clay had cast up the Compromise Act of 1833, to resist the rush of the nullifying tide, and doubtless saved the protective policy from utter ruin; but it is not improbable, that behind the breakwater of that compromise, during the quiet of general acquiescence in that measure, if we should inquire carefully, we should find that Webster's vigorous championship of the tariff during this period was one of the great preparatives, and perhaps the greatest of all the preparatives, for that tariff of 1842, one of the most stimulating and effective which this country has ever seen. And for those three July days of 1846, against the injurious and iniquitous Walker Tariff, Webster stood like Gibraltar, conspicuous and formidable, with amply stored subterranean arsenal and magazine, and with long bristling lines of fulminating guns.

3. In conclusion, it may be truthfully said that none of the great tariff speeches of the present day — not even the master pieces of McKinley, Reed, Hoar, Lodge, Blaine or Dingley, though many of them are more comprehensive and complete, surpasses

or even equals the Cyclopean massiveness of Webster's more fragmentary building. All the speeches that were made upon the other side now read like temporizing trickery in contrast with his majestic treatment of enduring principles. And no one can read his speeches without being impressed by their prophetic as well as their historic character and by the intimate relationship of the tariff to all the great facts of our national life—to the Revolution, the more perfect Union under the Constitution, the Civil War, the unequalled industrial development of the Republican *régime*, and the renaissance of sectionalism—the " continuation of the Rebellion" as Senator Sherman calls it—which characterizes the Wilson-Voorhees-Gorman propositions of 1894. Webster took it all in, and whoever understands Webster understands the tariff.

www.ingramcontent.com/pod-product-compliance
Lightning Source LLC
Chambersburg PA
CBHW021555270326
41931CB00009B/1231

* 9 7 8 3 3 3 7 3 9 7 8 3 8 *